Eric Dickerson

By
Nancy J. Nielsen

CRESTWOOD HOUSE

Mankato, Minnesota
U.S.A.

LIBRARY OF CONGRESS CATALOGING IN PUBLICATION DATA

Nielsen, Nancy J.
  Eric Dickerson
  SUMMARY: A biography of Los Angeles running back Eric Dickerson.
  1. Dickerson, Eric, 1960-   —Juvenile literature. 2. Football players—United
States—Biography—Juvenile literature. 3. Los Angeles Rams (Football team)—
Juvenile literature. [1. Dickerson, Eric, 1960-   . 2. Football players. 3. Afro-
Americans—Biography.] I. Title. II. Series
  GV939.D52N54   1988   796.332'092'4—dc19   [B]   [92]   87-27560
  ISBN 0-89686-366-2

        International Standard   Library of Congress
          Book Number: Catalog Card Number:
           0-89686-366-2   87-27560

PHOTO CREDITS

Cover: AP/Wide World Photos (Susan Ragan)
Globe Photos, Inc.: 33; (Scott Cunningham) 15; (Ralph Dominguez) 34
Focus on Sports: 10, 13, 16, 22, 23, 25, 26, 31, 36-37, 38, 42, 43
Focus West: (Rick Stewart) 4, 21
UPI/Bettmann News Photos: 18-19, 28-29, 44-45
AP/Wide World Photos: 47; (Charlie Bennett) 7; (Nick Ut) 40

Produced by Carnival Enterprises.

CRESTWOOD HOUSE

Box 3427, Mankato, MN, U.S.A. 56002

TABLE
OF
CONTENTS

A FAMOUS FOOTBALL STAR

Who is Eric Dickerson? He is a National Football League star running back!

In 1984, Eric broke O.J. Simpson's single-season rushing record of 2,003 yards in one season. Simpson had held the record for 11 years.

Then, in one game against the Houston Oilers, he rushed 215 yards. He broke O.J.'s record during that game. His total for the season was 2,105 yards!

Eric is fast, and he is smooth. He loves to run. When he runs during a game, he holds onto the ball, finds a hole in the defense, and runs hard. He is a player who is tough to stop.

FAMILY TIES

Eric was born on September 2, 1960, in Sealy, Texas. Sealy is a small town about 50 miles from Houston. Eric still goes to Sealy often to visit his mother.

The woman Eric calls "mom" is really his great aunt, Viola Dickerson. She raised Eric, adopting him when he was only three months old.

Eric's real mom, Helen, was also raised by Viola. Helen was only 17 years old when Eric was born. She was not married to Eric's father, Richard Seal. So both Helen and Viola agreed that Viola should raise Eric.

Eric Dickerson as a Los Angeles Ram.

This didn't matter to Eric. He still loved both Helen and Viola. But whenever Eric talks about his mother, he is referring to Viola, the woman who raised him.

According to Eric, his mom was the greatest single influence in his life. "Every time I've been faced with a major decision," Eric wrote in his book, *On the Run,* "I've made it a point to get my mother's input. I value my mom's opinion because I value her sense of what's important... she knows a lot about life."

Eric's father, Richard Seal, lives in Houston. Richard also played football as a running back for Prairie View College in Texas. Perhaps Eric inherited some of his running ability from Richard.

Eric had lots of friends while growing up in Sealy. He went to school in a town where, he said, blacks and whites were friendly to each other.

"I grew up together with white kids," Eric remembers. "I played with them and I argued with them, just as I did with black kids. I hung out at their houses, knew their brothers and sisters. It all seemed perfectly natural—I never gave it a second thought."

As a young boy, Eric was skinny and wore glasses. Some of the neighborhood kids used to pick on him. Even his friends teased him about his funny "egg-shaped" head.

Today Eric takes it all in stride. A good sense of humor has helped him. "Being black I always liked," he joked. "Being black and blue I could do without."

Perhaps it was because Eric loved his mom so much that he was teased. His mom used to go with him everywhere

Chicago Bear Walter Payton (right) and Eric joke with reporters at a press conference.

to make sure he stayed out of trouble.

"It's not that my mom didn't trust me," said Eric. "She just wasn't sure about some of the other kids. She didn't want me running in a bad crowd, picking up their habits."

According to Eric, Viola was good at giving spankings. "The thought of another burning behind was all the incentive I needed to stay in line," he recalled.

Today Eric is glad for the upbringing he received. Although his life has changed a lot, he feels his values and ethics are still intact. He's also glad he was raised in a quiet town, without the pressures and situations city kids often face, including drugs.

"I don't take drugs," Eric said. "Never even tried them, not even once, and I never will." During the off season, he works with young people to help them stay away from drugs.

THE YOUNG ATHLETE

When Eric was in the seventh and eighth grades, he started to play running back. "I'll never forget our first game," he said. "I was absolutely terrified, really just running for my life, but I guess my fear was a pretty good motivator. I wound up scoring four touchdowns that day. I liked that. Suddenly people were looking at me differently. Their eyes showed respect."

Baseball, too, was important to Eric in junior high school. He played center field, and dreamed of becoming either a baseball or a football star. But because football took up so much of his time in high school, he had to stop playing baseball.

Eric was also a track star in junior and senior high school. He could run the 100-yard dash in 9.4 seconds. He was a faster runner than anyone else in school, and won the state championship.

Even back then, Eric's coaches thought he was talented. They said he had "good eyes." They did not mean he had good eyesight, but that he could "see" what was happening on the football field.

"It was almost like a sixth sense," Eric recalled. "Instinctively, I could feel where the right place to run was...I can see things that other runners might not."

PROBLEMS WITH THE COACH

Even though Eric was a great high school football player, his life was not always easy. He did not get along with the football coach, Ralph Harris.

"I couldn't stand him sometimes," said Eric. "He rode us too hard. He always said we were a bunch of losers. I couldn't stand that."

Harris believed in lots of rules. He made his players wear short hair and did not allow Afros or cornrows. Players could not wear chains or jewelry. He inspected lockers and demanded neatness.

Once, Harris suspended Eric from all sports including football. Eric, who also played on the basketball team, had gotten into a fight with another basketball player.

It wasn't until Eric attended what the coach called "sunrise services"—strenuous morning exercises—that Harris changed his mind and allowed Eric to play football his senior year.

Today Harris, a college football coach, says he overdid the discipline with Eric. "I demanded what I thought it took to become a champion," Harris said. "I tried to take away (Eric's) individuality...I was very young and had a lot to learn."

Eric admits that he and his friends were not blameless. "There were times when we purposely did little things to irk Ralph, to see if he could take it as well as he dished it out," Eric said.

During Eric's senior year, the two finally apologized to each other. After that, they didn't have any problems. Today, Eric says he has no hard feelings towards Harris. He even thinks Harris helped him to become a better football player.

With Eric's help, the Sealy football team went on that year to become the Class AA state champions. Eric gained 2,642 yards and made 37 touchdowns during his senior year. Some people thought he was the best high school running back in the nation. Many college scouts wanted to persuade Eric to come and play on their team.

Sometimes as many as 12 scouts would come to Sealy and watch Eric play football. With so many colleges after him, his life became very hectic. Which school should he attend?

When he was in college, scouts began to notice Eric's talent.

CHOOSING SMU

Eric liked the Oklahoma Sooners. They were winners. Their coach, Barry Switzer, did not seem to have a lot of rules. Instead, he seemed friendly and fun to be around. Lots of Texas boys played on the team.

But Eric's mom did not want him to go to Oklahoma. She wanted him to stay in Texas. She liked the coach from Southern Methodist University (SMU). She thought Eric should go to college there.

Finally, Eric decided to go to SMU. "My heart wasn't really in it, though," Eric explained. "I did it for one reason only: out of respect for my mother."

The first couple of years, Eric was not happy at SMU. Some of the other football players did not like him because of all the attention he received.

During his sophomore year, the coaches made Eric and another player named Craig James take turns playing tailback on every offensive possession. Reporters called that plan the "Pony Express."

Eric did not like being what he thought was a part-time player. He wanted to be out there on every play. He wanted to carry the ball as often as he could. But looking back, Eric thinks that plan might have saved his knees for the pros.

During Eric's junior year at SMU he gained 1,428 yards and scored 19 touchdowns. During his senior year, he gained 1,617 yards and scored 17 touchdowns. He was

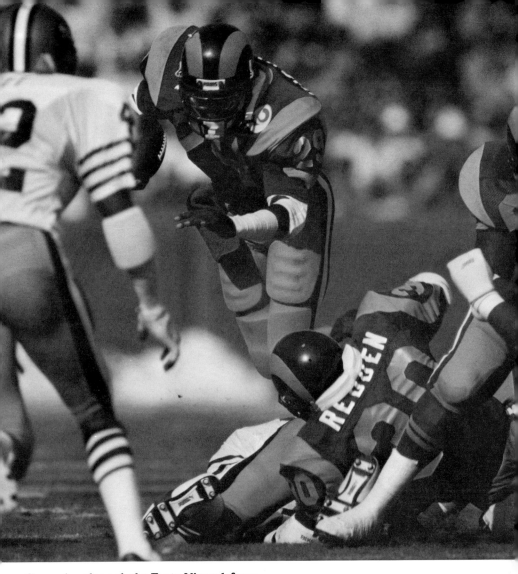

Squeezing through the Forty Niner defense.

voted Offensive Player of the Year in the Southwest
Conference. He was also chosen to be an All-American
player, and was third choice for the Heisman Trophy. Better
still, SMU won the Cotton Bowl during Eric's senior year.

THE LOS ANGELES RAMS

The National Football League (NFL) draft was coming up in April. Eric, now a senior, had his heart set on playing for the Los Angeles Rams. But many other pro football teams wanted Eric, also.

The NFL rules state that the team in last place at the end of the previous season has first choice in the draft. In 1983, the Rams had third pick.

The Baltimore Colts would pick first. Eric knew they wanted John Elway. But the Houston Oilers had second pick. What if they chose Eric before he had a chance to be drafted by the Rams?

The Rams knew Eric wanted to play for them, and so they made a deal with the Oilers. The Oilers could choose two players if they would trade places with the Rams. Then the Rams could pick second. They could pick Eric. And that's just what happened.

That wasn't the end, though, for Eric. A new football league, called the United States Football League (USFL), also wanted him. The Los Angeles Express, a USFL team, offered Eric a lot of money if he would play for them. It was much more than the Rams were going to pay him. Eric had a difficult decision to make.

He called his mother in Sealy, of course. She thought about it. Then she told him. "Go with the NFL. They've

The Los Angeles Rams drafted Eric in 1983.

been around a lot longer than that other league. At least you know they'll be there."

Eric listened to his mother's advice. He signed with the Rams that very same day.

A ROOKIE PLAYER

One of the reasons Eric wanted to play for the Rams was that he liked their coach, John Robinson. The first day of practice, though, Coach Robinson didn't think Eric was running hard enough. He kept yelling at him to run faster.

Despite a pile-up, Eric breaks free and runs with the ball.

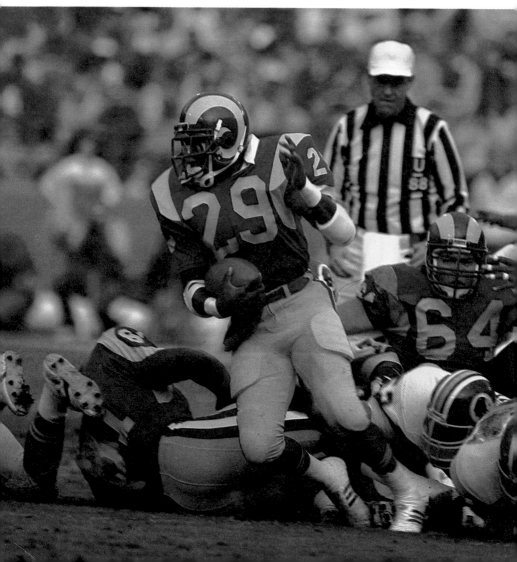

Eric was confused. He was running as fast as he could. Later he found out that Robinson thought Eric could run faster because he ran so smoothly. Most fast backs, according to Robinson, are not smooth. They make lots of noise when they run. When Eric runs, he hardly makes any noise at all.

Since the first day of practice, Eric's relationship with Robinson has been excellent. "John is always saying nice things about his players," Eric said. He thinks Robinson's best strength is motivating his players.

"It doesn't matter if you're the team's best player or the third-string punter, John will have you believing you're headed for the Hall of Fame," Eric said. "That's important, because football players have doubts and fears just like anyone else. John makes you feel invincible."

Eric likes the other Ram players, too. That doesn't mean they didn't tease him when he was a rookie. At first they called him "Number One" because he was the number-one draft choice. Later they called him Mr. Benny because he lived in a small apartment without much furniture. They thought he was like the comedian Jack Benny who was known for being cheap!

All that was okay, because Eric was right where he wanted to be. He was a running back for the Los Angeles Rams. Now all he had to do was prove himself.

He was terrified before his first game, a scrimmage against the Dallas Cowboys. "I was so jittery my mind went completely blank," Eric recalled. "I couldn't remember a thing—not a play, not a formation, not anything."

During his rookie year, Eric showed the team that he was fast and tough.

Fortunately, running back coach Bruce Snyder helped calm him down, and Eric made it through the game.

Later, during a game against the Green Bay Packers, Eric fumbled the ball and the Packers recovered it. The Packers won the game. Eric thought it was his fault.

But instead of letting a bad play get him down, Eric kept playing hard. He did his best. Soon it looked as if his rookie year was going to be better than he ever dreamed it could be.

During a game against the New York Jets, he ran 85 yards for a touchdown. He gained 192 yards for the whole game. In a later game against the Detroit Lions, Dickerson rushed 199 yards.

Eric's goal for his rookie year had been to gain 1,200 yards and make six touchdowns. Instead, he gained 1,808 yards with nine 100-yard games, and he scored 20 touchdowns. He rushed more yards than anyone else in the NFL that year. He was chosen the NFL Rookie of the Year!

BREAKING O.J.'S RECORD

1984 was Eric's best year to date. It was the year he rushed more yards in one season than any other running back in the history of the NFL.

A quick step to the left just might avoid a tackle.

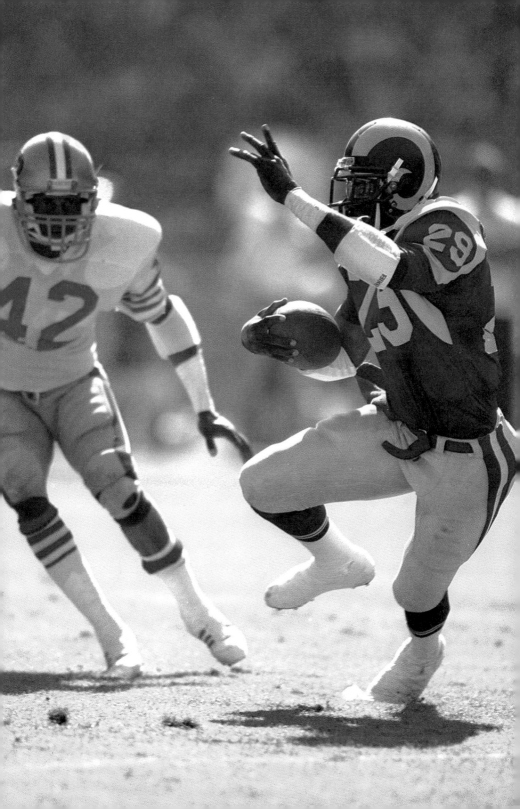

1984 was a terrific year for Eric.

Many people were watching him that year to see if he could break O.J. Simpson's record of 2,003 yards. Even The Juice himself, now a sportscaster for ABC News, was

In his second year with the Rams, Eric gained more and more yards.

watching. He had held the record for 11 years, but he could see that Dickerson was good.

"He can be the best ever," Simpson said.

Eric felt pressure from his fans and from reporters. Everyone was watching him to see if he could do it. In a game against New Orleans on December 2, Eric only rushed 149 yards. He was disappointed in himself. He thought he would have done better if he hadn't felt so much pressure.

Three days later, Eric had a dream — really a nightmare. He dreamed he rushed only 2,001 yards that season, two yards less than the record!

Then, on December 16, the Rams played the Houston Oilers. Before the game, the Oilers tried to give him a hard time. They told the newspapers that Eric was just an average player. They said his good record was due to the Ram offensive linemen. This made Eric angry.

It was war at Anaheim Stadium the day of the game. Eric thought the Oilers were playing dirty. "(They) were twisting my neck and ankles, hitting me after the whistle, diving onto pile-ups," he said. Fights broke out on the field.

Maybe being angry helped Eric. He was playing great football. By half time, he had already rushed 106 yards!

The other Ram players wanted their star running back to break O.J.'s record, too. But Ram offensive tackle Bill Bain saw how many yards Eric had gained by half time. He said to Ram guard Denny Harrah, "Let's go get him the other 106."

Eric kept gaining more and more yards. Soon it was the fourth quarter. The scoreboard lit up with the message, "ERIC DICKERSON HAS NOW RUSHED FOR 200 YARDS IN TODAY'S GAME." He needed only 12 more

This time the defense won!

There's just no way to avoid this tackle.

yards to break the record!

Then Eric took a hand-off and scored another touchdown! The fans were going wild. Six more yards and Dickerson would break O.J.'s record!

Time was running out, and the Oilers had the ball. But the Rams were determined that Eric break the record. They didn't want to wait until the next game.

Ram tight end David Hill was shouting, "Hey, we're going to get the record today. Let's get it out of the way."

"Get us the ball!" yelled Ram center Doug Smith. "Come on, stop them and get us the ball!"

The Oilers tried very hard to hold on to the ball until the game was over. Instead, Ram player Vince Newsome jumped up and intercepted a pass. The ball now belonged to the Rams!

The Rams formed a huddle. They were all very excited. Quarterback Jeff Kemp called the play. It was a play that would give Eric a chance to run with the ball.

The play worked. Eric got the ball, found a hole, and ran. He gained nine yards before the Oilers could stop him. The record had been broken!

Eric gained a total of 215 yards in 27 carries that game. By the end of the season, he had rushed 379 times for 2,105 yards and 14 touchdowns. He also caught 21 passes for 139 yards.

Now Eric was famous. His picture appeared on the cover of *Sports Illustrated*. An article inside told all about the great game he had played against the Oilers.

Eric breaks away from a Dallas Cowboy safety to gain yardage.

REWARDING HIS LINEMEN

Even though Eric got most of the attention as running back, he did not forget the 10 offensive linemen who made his record-breaking season possible.

He ordered 10 gold rings, each with the number 2,105 on it. Each ring also held 25 small diamonds. Then Eric presented them to the Ram linemen at a special dinner in their honor.

Offense is an "11-man proposition," Eric believed. He could not have broken the record without the help of all the other players. "We had broken O.J.'s record as a team, an accomplishment shared together," Dickerson wrote in his book. "It was a tremendous thrill, a once-in-a-lifetime feeling."

The linemen wanted to do something special, too. They came up with a plan that would help victims of a famine in Africa. They promised to each give $1 to the relief fund for every yard Eric gained in 1985.

Just another routine run with the ball.

"JUST SAY NO" TO DRUGS

Because Eric was famous, he got lots of attention in the newspapers and on TV. He decided to use his fame for good, and he accepted many invitations to do charity work.

One person who asked for his help was First Lady Nancy Reagan. Nancy Reagan was working hard to help kids stay away from drugs through her "Just Say No To Drugs" campaign.

Eric started a "Just Say No" chapter in Los Angeles. He met with children ages 6-17 at local parks. There he talked with them about the harmful effects of drugs. He encouraged them to stay away from drugs.

"Since athletes are heroes to today's children, I feel it's their moral responsibility to stay clean from drugs," Eric said. "Some people think that athletes shouldn't be held up as role models, that it isn't fair. Well, fair or not, the fact remains that we are looked upon as role models. And we've got to act accordingly."

Many children from Los Angeles were anxious to join the club. They were called Dickerson's Rangers and wore Dickerson T-shirts with the number 2,105 on them. Sometimes the Rangers were bused to home games to watch Eric play football.

Eric hopes to work with the Rangers for many years. He likes working with kids and helping them with their problems. The Dickerson Rangers, he feels, are doing a lot

During his time off the football field, Eric meets with the Dickerson's Rangers.

of good in Los Angeles. "If I can help one person give up drugs, or never try them," he said, "then I've accomplished a lot."

MONEY PROBLEMS

Eric missed training camp and the first two games of the 1985 season. He refused to play until the Rams offered him more money. When he first signed with the Rams he had agreed to play for $350,000 a year. That's a lot of money, but many professional football players make much more than that.

Eric knew he could not play football forever. What if an injury cut his career short? He knew he could be cut in the middle of the season, and not paid another cent. So he wanted to make as much money as he could in 1985.

After Eric waited 47 days, the Rams finally offered him a contract he liked. The contract was reportedly for about $800,000 a year. Now he was ready to play ball.

Even though his teammates still call him Mr. Benny, Eric no longer deserves to be called that. He has bought a large house in Irvine, California. He is not married, but says he would like to be someday.

Eric also built a new house for Viola in Sealy, Texas. He installed a satellite dish for her TV so she can watch all of his football games!

Stepping out in style.

This running back knows his job—avoid the defense!

THE 1985 SEASON

Some people thought Eric would not play as well in 1985 because he missed training camp. But Coach Robinson wasn't worried, as long as Eric reported in shape.

Because he was such a talented runner, the Rams planned their strategy around him. "Our whole blocking scheme is set up to let me run anywhere I can," Eric told a reporter. "I can take the ball anywhere, inside or outside, penetrate or go to the sideline."

The Rams made it to the playoffs that year. They faced the Dallas Cowboys. Eric played a great game. During the second half, he broke away from the Dallas defense and ran 55 yards for a touchdown.

Eric gained 248 yards in that one game. No one had ever run for more yards against the Cowboys. No running back had ever gained more yards against any team in a playoff game.

"If there's one team in the league that I really like to beat, it's the Dallas Cowboys," Eric said. "I guess it goes back to when I was in college, living in Dallas. I got so fed up with hearing how great the Cowboys were. Even if they were great, I was a Rams' fan and didn't want to hear it. I always said that I would love to face the Cowboys and have a great game. That playoff game was my chance, and I did it."

The Rams met the Chicago Bears at the next playoff game. Eric remembers getting hit hard by Bear defenseman Mike Singletary in the second quarter.

"I never saw him coming and he really got me good, right in the face with the front of his helmet," said Eric. "It was like my body went into shock. I'll never forget it. It was one of the hardest hits of my career."

The Rams lost the game to the Bears, 24-0. Still, they finished the season with an 11-5 winning record. Eric rushed 1,234 yards that season and made 12 touchdowns.

Eric gained 248 yards in a 1985 game with the Dallas Cowboys.

ERIC VERSUS HERSHEL WALKER

In the spring of 1985, a running back in the newly-formed USFL rushed 2,411 yards—306 more yards than Eric's 2,105 NFL record. His name was Hershel Walker.

The NFL season is 16 games long. Walker, in the USFL, played in an 18-game season. Nevertheless, he broke the record during his season's 16th game. Many sports fans began to debate who was the better football player, Walker or Dickerson.

The two players are very different. Walker weighs 225 pounds, five pounds more than Eric. Walker is two inches shorter—6'1" compared with Eric's 6'3". He is also two years younger than Eric.

What did Eric think of all the who-is-better talk? The USFL is only a "minor" league, he told reporters, and records set in that league cannot be compared with NFL records.

Only time will tell. In 1986, Hershel Walker signed with Eric's old rival, the Dallas Cowboys!

A lucky fan gets an autograph.

THE 1986 SEASON

In 1986, Eric was still at the top of the list in the NFL for rushing. He gained 1,821 yards that season and scored 11 touchdowns.

The Rams had some problems, though. They were last on the list for passes completed. They did not make it to the Super Bowl that year.

The top NFL rusher keeps on running.

Despite team problems, Eric was the Rams most important player in 1986.

Eric made some mistakes in an important playoff game against the Washington Redskins. He fumbled the ball three times. The Rams lost the game. But Eric made no excuses.

"We could have won this game," he said, "but we turned the ball over. I turned the ball over. We beat ourselves."

Even so, he remained the Rams most important player. Without Eric, they could not have held on to a winning record in 1986.

The Dallas Cowboys have a hard time stopping Eric—he's on his way to a touchdown!

PROBLEMS IN 1987

Early in the 1987 season, problems began to mount for Eric. He became involved in a contract dispute with the Rams.

And after two games of the regular season, the National Football League Players Association declared a strike. The strike went on for four weeks. Three of the missed games were played by replacement players.

Just after the strike ended, a bombshell dropped on the sports world. The Rams traded Eric Dickerson to the Indianapolis Colts!

LOOKING AHEAD

Eric is one of the most exciting runners in NFL history. He feels he has many good years of play ahead. Eric thinks the Indianapolis Colts have the potential to become a great football team, and he is looking forward to being a part of that bright picture.

Eric Dickerson—charging ahead with the Indianapolis Colts!

ERIC DICKERSON'S PROFESSIONAL STATISTICS

		Rushing			
		Total	Avg.	Longest	
Year	No.	Yards	Gain	Gain	TD
1983	390	1,808	4.6	85t*	18
1984	379	2,105	5.6	66	14
1985	292	1,234	4.2	43	12
1986	404	1,821	4.5	42t	11
Totals	1,465	6,968	4.7	85t	55
		Pass Receiving			
1983	51	404	7.9	37t	2
1984	21	139	6.7	19	0
1985	20	126	6.3	33	2
1986	26	205	7.9	28	0
Totals	118	874	7.2	37t	4

Playoffs

		Rushing			
1985	51	294	5.8	55t	2
		Pass Receiving			
1985	4	6	1.5	1.5	0

*Touchdown scored on play